Forgiven Forever

BOB GEORGE

HARVEST HOUSE PUBLISHERS
Eugene, Oregon 97402

FORGIVEN FOREVER

Taken from **CLASSIC CHRISTIANITY**
Copyright © 1989 by Harvest House Publishers
Eugene, Oregon 97402

ISBN 0-89081-803-7

CONTENTS

1

Forgiven to Be Filled

Several years ago in Canada I had just completed a seminar lecture on God's forgiveness when a man approached me. He looked about 60 years old, but it was hard to be sure because of his haggard appearance. His eyes were dull and lifeless, his face was covered with deep creases leading down to his slack mouth, and his shoulders were stooped. When he spoke, his voice came forth in a low drone.

"Mr. George," he said, "I really want to believe that God forgives me, but I don't seem to be able to accept it. How can you know that God forgives your sins?"

"Edward, I just spoke for over an hour on God's total forgiveness in Christ. Were you here for the lecture?"

"Yes, I heard what you said, but I just can't believe that God really forgives me." Wondering if Edward was really a Christian, I took some time to find out. He told of how he had accepted Christ as his Savior and Lord at a very early age. Edward's understanding and answers were all solid regarding his personal faith in Christ: He knew beyond a shadow of a doubt that Christ lived in him, and that he was going to spend eternity in heaven after his death. The source of his doubts had to lie elsewhere.

5

"How long have you been struggling with these doubts about God's forgiveness?" I asked him.

"Ever since I was a child," Edward said sadly. "When I was young, I did something *very wrong*. Every day since then I have begged God to forgive me, but I just can't believe that He has."

I could hardly believe my ears. "Edward, how old are you?"

"Sixty-two."

"Do you mean to tell me that you have been begging God to forgive you for over 50 years?"

He looked me in the eyes with that helpless expression and nodded. "I should have been serving Him for those 50 years, but I have wasted my life. That's why I'm asking you if you think God could ever forgive me."

At the time, I thought that Edward's was a unique story. I have since come to know that many, many Christians share the same bondage. They have committed some sin that seems to be ever a part of their present, even as the years roll by. It is constantly on their minds, like an ever-present black cloud hanging over them.

A Christian like this will never mature. He will never, as long as he is held in the bondage of guilt over a past sin, experience all that Christ has intended for us to experience through His indwelling life. Let me express this in a straightforward manner: *Until you rest in the finality of the cross, you will never experience the reality of the resurrection.*

Second Peter 1:3-9 is a passage that perfectly illustrates this principle. It begins with this incredible news:

His divine power has given us *everything we need for life and godliness* through our knowledge of Him who called us by His own glory and goodness. Through these He has given us His very great and precious promises, so that through them *you may participate in the divine nature* and escape the corruption in the world caused by evil desires (verses 3,4).

So many Christians start out with Jesus Christ, then go looking for something better, some kind of "advanced Christianity." We will stray into all kinds of tangents looking for the "something more" that will transform our dull existence into spiritual reality. Sometimes it's a desire for something "deeper." But 2 Peter 1:3 says that we have received how many things? It says "*everything* we need for life and godliness."

I was teaching this recently on a call-in radio program and was asked this question by a listener: "If it is true, as you say, that every Christian has received everything he needs, then why don't many Christians experience it? Even Christians who know about Christ living in them?" (To be specific, someone like Edward.) Let's continue in the passage in 2 Peter 1. After teaching that we have everything we need in Christ, Peter exhorts his readers to press on to maturity in verses 5-8:

For this very reason, make every effort to add to your faith, goodness;

and to goodness, knowledge; and to knowledge, self-control; and to self-control, perseverance; and to perseverance, godliness; and to godliness, brotherly kindness; and to brotherly kindness, love. For if you possess these qualities in increasing measure, they will keep you from being ineffective and unproductive in your knowledge of our Lord Jesus Christ.

No one attains these qualities at a single stroke. They are marks of maturity that we will be growing in as we learn to live by faith in the indwelling Lord Jesus Christ. But what about an Edward? "Ineffective" and "unproductive" are two words that describe his life pretty accurately. What is it that can block this process of maturity from happening? The answer is given in verse 9: "But if anyone does not have them, he is nearsighted and blind, *and has forgotten that he has been cleansed from his past sins.*"

There's the answer! Failure to recognize and trust that the sin issue between you and God is over will effectively stop your spiritual growth in Christ. It's really not complicated. The process of spiritual maturity is simply our learning to turn more and more areas of our lives over to Christ through faith. The past is over; the future isn't here yet. Therefore, living by faith can only be done in the *present*.

If Satan, on the other hand, can keep us preoccupied with the *past* through dredging up our feelings of guilt over past sins, then we can never be free to trust Christ as we walk through life today. Besides, how can we trust Christ with our lives if we are unsure of His attitude toward us? Most of us have been taught from an early age that God is holy and "hates sin." If I have committed sins, how can I approach Him with confidence?

The only solution is an understanding of, and a total trust in, the fact that Jesus Christ did it all at the cross; that the sin issue between man and God is truly over. We must come to the biblical conviction that the forgiveness of our sins is not just some "heavenly bookkeeping" that will enable us to slip into heaven some day; God's forgiveness is a *present reality* that enables us to concentrate on walking daily with a loving and accepting God who desires to live through us. Ephesians 1:7 says, *"In Him we have* redemption through His blood, *the forgiveness of sins,* in accordance with the riches of God's grace." Forgiveness is not something we might have, or have on some days and not on others; forgiveness is something the Christian lives in continually, just like we live in and breathe the air. "In Him, we *have* . . . the forgiveness of sins." It is written in the *present tense*.

What a tragedy to look at a man like Edward who believed that he had wasted his life because of a single past failure. He was in bondage because of error; the solution was truth.

"Edward," I said, "did any of your children ever do anything wrong?"

"Well, yes, many times."

"Did you forgive them?"

"Yes, of course."

"Edward, what if on one of those occasions when your child did something wrong, you forgave him, and he refused to believe you, but came every day bringing up the subject again? 'Daddy, are you *sure* that you forgive me for that?' On and on, every day: 'Are you *sure* you forgive me, Daddy? Are you sure?' Tell me, Edward, as a father how would that make you feel?"

Edward creased his brow in a pained expression. "It would break my heart," he said.

"Then, Edward, don't you think it's about time you stopped breaking the heart of God? Don't you think it's about time you stopped insulting the Spirit of God who has written dozens of promises in the Bible that teach that He has forgiven *all* your sins, once and for all?

"Edward, look at this," I said. I pointed him to Colossians 2:13,14:

> When you were dead in your sins and in the uncircumcision of your sinful nature, God made you alive with Christ. He forgave us *all* our sins, having cancelled the written code, with its regulations, that was against us and that stood opposed to us; He took it away, nailing it to the cross.

"According to this," I continued, "how forgiven are you in God's sight?"

"Totally," he answered.

"Does God hold any accusations against you?"

"No."

"Do you see why?" I asked. "It's so that you can concentrate on the other half of the gospel, that 'God made you *alive* with Christ.' You've been totally preoccupied with the thing that God is *finished* dealing with—sin—with the result that you've totally neglected what God is trying to do with you *today*—teach you about life!

"Edward, don't you see that every one of us would be doomed except for the unbelievable mercy and grace of God? He had to do it all because we were totally helpless to do anything for ourselves. He knows all about you and your deepest failures. What He wants you to do is to rest in what He has done through the cross—to put it to bed once and for all—so that you can begin to experience what He has done through the resurrection."

Edward looked long and hard at Colossians 2:13,14 in my Bible. Finally he said, "I'd like to pray." Closing his eyes, Edward prayed, "Lord Jesus. All these years I've thought that You hated me because of my failure. I've asked and begged You to forgive me over and over, and I have seen myself as a total failure. But today I'm going to start trusting in Your promise. You have heard me ask You to forgive my sin for the last time. I won't insult You and Your grace again. Now, from this day on, Lord, teach me what it means that You live in me. In the years that I have left, I'm Yours to use however You want."

Through seeing and trusting in the completeness of Christ's work on the cross to deal with our sins, Edward finally became free to experience the life of Christ, which had in fact been his since his conversion many years before. His life perfectly illustrates the principle of 2 Peter 1:9: Until you rest in the finality of the cross, you will never experience the reality of the resurrection.

Satan has done a masterful job of keeping the Christian world preoccupied with the thing that God has dealt with once and for all—sin—and ignorant of the thing that God wants us to be preoccupied with—life! This in no way means that we are to minimize what Jesus did on the cross. Thank God for that! But it is only when we understand that the ultimate goal of salvation was the restoration of life that we can truly appreciate the purpose and meaning of Jesus Christ's death for us on the cross.

The process of canning is an excellent illustration of the two parts of the gospel. Let's say that you are going to preserve some peaches. What is the first thing you have to do? Sterilize the jars. Why the process of sterilization? So that the contents of the jars—the peaches—will be preserved from spoiling.

Imagine a husband coming home and finding his wife boiling jars in the kitchen. "What are you doing, honey?"

"Sterilizing jars."

"Why are you doing that?" the husband asks.

"I just like clean jars," she answers.

The husband is clearly at a loss. "What are you going to do next?" he asks.

"Keep them clean!"

This story doesn't make much sense, does it? You have never seen anyone decorate his kitchen with a sterile jar collection. No, the only reason to sterilize jars is *because you intend to put something in them.* We would never expect to find a person involved in only half the process of canning, just cleansing jars. But we have done this exact thing with the gospel! We have separated God's sterilization process—the cross—from His filling process—Christ coming to live in us through His resurrection!

The Christian world, to a large extent, has been guilty of teaching half a gospel—that is, the cross of Christ which brought us forgiveness of sins. But by separating forgiveness of sins from the message of receiving the life of Christ, we have not only missed out on experiencing life, but we have lost sight of the purpose of forgiveness in the first place. The reason that God had to deal once and for all with the sin issue was so that we could be filled with Christ "without spoiling."

As a matter of fact, there is one final part of the canning process. After sterilizing the jars and filling them with fruit, the jars are *sealed.* Sealing keeps the good things inside and the bad things that would spoil the contents outside. We read in Ephesians 1:13:

> And you also were included in Christ when you heard the word of truth, the gospel of your salvation. Having believed, you were marked in Him with a *seal*, the promised Holy Spirit.

Cleansing, filling, and sealing: a wonderful

picture of salvation! Once we see that the goal of salvation is the raising of dead men to life, it is easy to see why Christ had to deal with the sin issue once and for all. This is exactly what the New Testament teaches from beginning to end. For example, notice these verses from three different writers:

> The death He died, He died to sin *once for all*; but the life He lives, He lives to God (Romans 6:10).

> But now He has appeared *once for all* at the end of the ages to do away with sin by the sacrifice of Himself (Hebrews 9:26).

> For Christ died for sins *once for all*, the righteous for the unrighteous, to bring you to God. He was put to death in the body but made alive by the Spirit (1 Peter 3:18).

The message of God's complete, 100-percent forgiveness in Christ has been a controversial, mind-boggling subject for nearly 2000 years. To prepare the way, God gave Israel the law of Moses with its sacrificial system. Even though these sacrifices were God-ordained, no one was ever made right with God through them. Instead, they were merely a picture of Christ and His finished work on our behalf:

> The law is only a shadow of the good things that are coming—not the

realities themselves. For this reason it can never, by the same sacrifices repeated endlessly year after year, make perfect those who draw near to worship (Hebrews 10:1).

Forgiveness was different under the law (also called the Old Covenant). It was a good news/bad news situation. Let's say that you are an Israelite living under the law. All year long God is keeping a record of your violations of the law, and the entire nation's as well. All year long you feel the guilt of your sins; you live in fear of God's punishment, which was threatened for transgressions of the law. But the great Day of Atonement is coming! The annual day of fasting and praying and confessing your sins. The day each year when the perfect bull is sacrificed on behalf of the nation. The one and only time that a single mortal man, representing the whole nation, can enter into the most holy room of the temple, the Holy of Holies, which represents the very presence of God. Taking sacrificial blood, the high priest fearfully enters behind the veil and there sprinkles the blood which covers the nation's—and your—sins for the previous year.

Two goats are sacrificed as well: One is slain at the altar; the other, called the scapegoat, becomes the subject of an unusual ceremony. Elders of the nation place their hands on the head of the goat, symbolizing the transfer of the nation's sins to the animal. Then, before thousands of witnesses lining the streets, the scapegoat is driven from the city, out into the wilderness, symbolizing the removal of your sins. You watch with relief and thanksgiving, the innocent animal symbolically taking your guilt away. What relief! That's the good news.

What's the bad news? Tomorrow your sins begin adding up again. Next year there will need to be another sacrifice. And the next year. And the next.

God graciously gave this system to Israel as a means for man to experience relief from the guilt he experienced under the law. The key Old Testament word is "atonement," which means a covering. Those sacrificial offerings did, indeed, *cover* sins, but they could not *take them away,* "because it is *impossible* for the blood of bulls and goats to *take away* sins" (Hebrews 10:4). A man under the law could enjoy the blessing of God's forgiveness, but that system provided no final solution. It is similar to the use of a credit card, which enables a person to have the benefit today of the stereo he wants to buy, without paying cash. That's the good news. But the bad news is that somebody is going to have to pay the tab! The card didn't pay for the stereo; it only transferred the debt to an account. That account will still have to be paid.

Then in God's perfect timing, Jesus Christ was introduced to Israel by John the Baptist: "Look, the Lamb of God who *takes away* the sin of the world!" (John 1:29). From that point on, the finished work of Christ is presented in the New Testament in total contrast to the old system:

> And by [God's] will, we have been
> made holy through the sacrifice of the

body of Jesus Christ *once for all.* Day after day every priest stands and performs his religious duties; again and again he offers the same sacrifices, which *can never take away sins.* But when this priest had offered *for all time one sacrifice* for sins, He sat down at the right hand of God (Hebrews 10:10-12).

Relentlessly the New Testament hammers home the message that Jesus Christ offered Himself as one sacrifice for all time. When will we believe it? In contrast to the Old Covenant priests who are pictured as "standing" and making continual sacrifices, Christ is shown as having *sat down.* Why is He seated? Because "*It is finished!*" (John 19:30). The writer of Hebrews reaches the climax of his argument in 10:14: "Because by *one sacrifice* He has made *perfect forever* those who are being made holy." Jesus Christ has done it all!

I find that few Christians can read that verse without flinching and trying to water it down. It is too bold, and the implications are too threatening. Notice that it doesn't say we *act* perfect; this is talking about identity. But the Bible says that *through Jesus Christ* we *have* been made totally acceptable in the eyes of a holy God!

I'll never forget a conversation I had several years ago with a pastor of a certain denomination that teaches that you can lose your salvation. The more we talked, the more obvious it became to me that this man really did have a good handle on the grace of God, at least intellectually. Finally I looked him right in the eye and said, "Jim, you know the Word of God. You also know how great a work our Lord did at the cross. I think you know too much to really believe that a born-again Christian can lose his salvation."

A sheepish, sly grin grew on Jim's face. Then he said, "You're right, Bob. Jesus Christ has done it all. There's nothing more that needs to be done or can be done to deal with man's sins. I do know that once you've been born again, you can't be unborn." Then he turned serious. "But how could I ever keep my people in line if I taught them that? They would just take that message as a license to sin. So I don't teach it."

I really wonder how many other leaders in church history have done the same thing out of abject fear of "what the people will do." The tragedy is that their fear is unnecessary—*if* they are teaching the entire gospel: not the cross and forgiveness of sins alone, but the cross plus God's gift of the resurrected life of Christ.

God said that in the New Covenant, "I will put My laws in their minds and write them on their hearts" (Hebrews 8:10). If salvation was only forgiveness of sins without a change of heart, yes, we would probably take it as a license to sin. But not when Christ lives in us! When we are learning to experience the "abundant life" that Jesus Christ has promised, we become preoccupied with our daily relationship with Him: the One who loved us and gave His life *for* us, so that He could give His life *to* us. But we absolutely have to settle the finality of the cross in our own minds, or we will never be free to discover, experience, and enjoy the reality of the resurrection—real *life* restored to man!

2

Putting the Pieces Together

After many years spent talking with people of
all denominations from every part of the country,
I picture the average Christian's understanding
to be much as mine was: like a person with a big
box of jigsaw puzzle pieces, each piece representing a Bible verse, a sermon illustration, or a
doctrine they have been taught. If you have been
a Christian very long at all, you have probably
accumulated quite a collection!

Have you ever tried to put together a jigsaw
puzzle without the cover of the box which shows
what the finished picture should look like? You
pick up a piece: "Well, it's got a little red, a little
green, and a little white in it. But I don't have a
clue to what it is." So you pick up another piece
that also has some red, green, or white. They
don't fit easily, but with a little brute force you
can make them stick together. Unfortunately,
the union of the two still doesn't look like anything recognizable.

On the other hand, if you have the cover of the
box to compare the piece to, you can easily identify where the piece goes. "Now I see," you say.
"The red on this piece is part of that barn, the
green is part of the tree, and the white is part of
the sheet hanging on the line. Oh, here's another

part of the barn, and it fits like so." How much easier it is to identify the small pieces when you can put them into a context! And that is exactly what God did for me, through opening my understanding to the "life and death" issue of salvation. He took me back to a bird's-eye view of the whole Bible, which immediately caused hundreds of small pieces that we call verses to fall into place. There weren't any new verses. I knew them all well. But finally I could see where they fit in—without having to apply brute force!

As I have had the pleasure of teaching thousands of people the same life-transforming truths, I have heard them say again and again, "For the first time in my life, I can understand my Bible!" They always say this with a sense of wonder. That shows you that they had, in their hearts, really given up hope of ever understanding the Word of God. A friend of mine said it this way: "It was astonishing to me to discover that Christianity actually makes sense!" That sounds strange, yet I have heard it repeatedly.

When people are challenged for the first time to examine their understanding of the gospel, there are many predictable questions that they will ask. The following account is a very typical discussion.

I was teaching a seminar when a man named Don said, "Bob, I've been taught that a Christian can lose his salvation. I know that Christ died for our *past* sins, but what about our *future* sins? I don't understand what you mean when you say that Christ *had* to take away *all* sins."

I answered him this way: "Don, let's take your questions in order. First of all, when Christ died for your sins, how many of them were in the future?"

He hesitated a moment. "All of them," he answered.

"They had to be, of course, unless you're more than 2000 years old!" I said, and we laughed. "The problem, Don, is that we are looking at things from the perspective of time, and God is looking at things from the perspective of eternity, which is entirely out of time. We look at the passing of days and years like we watch railroad cars at a crossing—one at a time. But God sees all of time as a person would see the entire train from an airplane overhead—from the engine to the caboose.

"At the cross, God took every sin that every man will ever commit and placed them all on Jesus Christ. The Lord Jesus took all the punishment for your and my sins in one action. That's why 1 John 2:2 (alternate rendering) says, 'He is the one who turns aside God's wrath, taking away our sins, and not only ours but also the sins of the whole world.' The theological word is 'propitiation.' Have you ever heard of it?"

"I don't even think I could pronounce it!" Don said. "What does that mean?"

"Propitiation means that God the Father was totally *satisfied* with the sacrifice made by His Son. There at the cross, God poured out every ounce of His anger and hatred for sin that you and I deserved so that His justice is totally *satisfied*; except that Jesus took it for us. That's why the Bible says, 'He did it to *demonstrate His justice* at the present time, so as to be *just* and *the one who justifies* the man who has faith in Jesus' (Romans 3:26). That's why there isn't any wrath left for you."

I could tell the group was thinking hard. "Let's think it through," I continued. "If you were to stand before the judgment seat of God today in your own righteousness, what would be the verdict?"

"Guilty," Don said.

"That's right, and it would be the same for me. Now then, what is the punishment for sin?"

"Death, I guess," Don answered again.

"That's right. Romans 6:23 says, 'For the wages of sin is death.' And Christ took it for you! That's why there isn't any punishment left for you.

"By the way," I continued, "I only quoted the first half of Romans 6:23. Not too many of us seem to know the second half: 'but the gift of God is eternal *life* in Christ Jesus our Lord.' This gets us into the second part of your question about why Christ had to totally deal with the sin issue. Let's imagine that a man has died of a disease—cancer, for example. Don, if you had the power to save the man, how many problems would you have to solve? Two! You'd have to raise him to life, but you'd also have to cure his cancer, wouldn't you?" I paused while they thought it over.

"For example," I went on, "what if you cured his cancer, but did nothing else?"

"He would still be dead," Don answered.

"That's right. You'd just have a healthy dead man on your hands!" Don and I laughed, and I continued. "On the other hand, what if you raised him to life without curing his cancer?"

After a moment's pause, Don answered, "He would just die again."

"You've got it. And that, Don, is a perfect picture of man's condition, from God's point of view, after the Fall. Ever since Adam sinned, the earth has been the land of the walking dead— spiritually dead. What is the disease that killed man? We've already seen it: 'The wages of sin is death.' So from God's point of view, salvation involves the raising of spiritually dead men to life. But before God could give life to the dead, He had to totally eradicate the fatal disease that killed men—sin. So the cross was God's method of dealing with the disease called sin, and the resurrection of Christ was and is God's method of giving life to the dead!"

Don was thoughtful for a minute. "Okay," he said, "I think I'm getting it."

The rest of the group had been quietly listening to this exchange, but Lynn raised her hand. "I'm still not sure why you can't lose your salvation," she said.

"All right," I answered, "let's first remember what salvation is. From our study, how would you explain it?"

"It's when a person trusts in the Lord Jesus and receives forgiveness of sins and His life," Lynn answered. "The Spirit of God comes to live in you."

"That's good," I said. "Now remember: Adam was created spiritually alive. What caused the Spirit of God to depart from Adam, leaving him spiritually dead?"

"His sin," was her answer.

"Right. Now, Jesus Christ on the cross experienced death, too. Why did He die?"

The group was more hesitant this time. Then Don spoke up, "I guess it was the same thing—sin."

"That's right," I answered. "Second Corinthians 5:21 says, 'God made Him who had no sin *to be sin* for us, so that in Him we might become the righteousness of God.' So we're left with this: Adam died because of his sin. Jesus Christ died because He *became* sin. How can you and I know that we will never die spiritually again, even though we still commit sins as Christians?"

Don was confident now as he answered. "Because the disease has been totally taken away. Our sins have been forgiven."

"Therefore," I concluded, "when the Lord Jesus gives us His resurrected life, it can truly be *eternal* life, because the only thing that could ever cause you to die—sin—has been completely dealt with at the cross. That's how you can know that your salvation is secure forever. Now, knowing that you are secure in Christ, you are free to concentrate on God's greatest priority for you today: learning to experience real life—Christ Himself living through you."

Discussions like these can be a little tough to wade through at times, but there are tremendous benefits. We Christians tend to talk too much in generalities, and this helps to cause the phenomenon where people can speak the Christian "language" but have never really thought through—for themselves, based on the Bible—what they believe. It's when we make ourselves take what the Bible says and carry it all the way to conclusions that we discover the experience that I mentioned earlier in the chapter—where Christianity really makes sense and it works in real life, in the real world.

In many cases, Christians' understanding of salvation is not so much *wrong* as *too small*. For example, most people are at least familiar with the word "forgiveness," but the Bible has much more to say about our salvation than forgiveness. One of the major biblical terms that expresses the finality of the sin issue is "reconciliation." It is expressed in 2 Corinthians 5:19: "God was *reconciling the world to Himself* in Christ, not counting men's sins against them. And He has committed to us the message of reconciliation."

The entire world has been reconciled to God through the cross. I read this verse on the radio, and it caused a listener named Bill to ask this question: "Bob, if the whole world is reconciled to God, does that mean that the whole world is saved?"

"That depends, Bill, on your definition of salvation. If salvation is just man's being reconciled to God, the answer would be yes. But that's not salvation, is it?"

After thinking for a moment, Bill said, "No, salvation is when a person receives Jesus Christ Himself; when he is born again."

"Right," I answered. "The word 'reconciliation' means that the barrier between God and man—sin—has been taken away. A bridge has been built between man and God. Therefore, the only thing that keeps any man from eternal life is his refusal to accept the salvation that God offers. That's why the only sin that will ever send a man to hell is his unbelief. John 3:18 says, 'Whoever believes in Him is not condemned, but whoever does not believe stands condemned already because he has not believed in the name of God's one and only Son.' What does it mean to be condemned already? He remains dead. Because of his sins? No. Because of his unbelief."

This is a shocking message! Many of us are used to thinking of a vengeful, furious God who is just itching to blast men off the face of the earth. But the gospel is actually the announcement of an *accomplished fact*—God's work of reconciliation has *already* taken place! And reconciliation is something that God did *on His own initiative*. He didn't consult anyone—He just did it.

People talk glibly about "man's search for God." But the gospel is the story of *God's search for man*! This is the fantastic message of Romans 5:6-10. The theme that is hit again and again is God's taking the initiative to bring about reconciliation with men:

> When we were still powerless, Christ died for the ungodly. . . . But God demonstrates His own love for us in this: While we were still sinners, Christ died for us. . . . When we were God's enemies, we were reconciled to Him through the death of His Son (Romans 5:6,8,10).

The familiar story of the prodigal son in Luke 15:11-32 gives a perfect picture of God's attitude toward the lost world since the cross. The young man has taken and squandered his inheritance, bringing shame to his father and family. Destitute, he has accepted the lowest possible job for a Jew, feeding filthy swine, in order to stay alive. He has really hit bottom. But what is his father's attitude? He hasn't written the boy off. That father isn't standing with his arms folded, glaring down the road and sputtering, "You just wait until I get my hands on that kid! He's going to pay for what he's done!" No! You can tell the father's attitude by his response when he saw his son returning:

> But while he was still a long way off, his father saw him and was filled with compassion for him; he ran to his son, threw his arms around him and kissed him (Luke 15:20).

The next thing he did was to throw a party. Now think about it. When that boy was still with the pigs, what stood in the way of his returning to his father? Nothing on the father's part! In fact it's easy to picture that man each day gazing down the road with a longing expression, thinking, "Maybe today my boy will come home." The only thing that kept that boy from his father was the son's own decision. Today, God is calling men to come home, just like the father longed for his prodigal son.

To many people, this emphasis on total forgiveness and Christ living in you seems threatening because they fear that it will lead people to become complacent about their Christian lives. They hear the phrase "living by faith" and picture lazy people sitting around, waiting for something to happen. The exact opposite is true. It is an emphasis on the cross and forgiveness of sins *to the exclusion of teaching people about sharing Christ's resurrected life* that really leads to complacency.

Let me share an illustration. Let's imagine that a king made a decree in his land that there would be a blanket pardon extended to all prostitutes. Would that be good news to you if you were a prostitute? Of course it would. No longer would you have to live in hiding, fearing the sheriff. No longer would you have a criminal record; all past offenses are wiped off the books. So the pardon would definitely be good news. But would it be any motivation at all for you to change your lifestyle? No, not a bit.

But let's go a little further with our illustration. Let's say that not only is a blanket pardon extended to all who have practiced prostitution, but the king has asked you, in particular, to become his bride. What happens when a prostitute marries a king? She becomes a queen. *Now* would you have a reason for a change of lifestyle? Absolutely. It doesn't take a genius to realize that the lifestyle of a queen is several levels superior to that of a prostitute. No woman in her right mind would go back to her previous life.

As long as a half-gospel continues to be taught, we are going to continue producing Christians who are very thankful that they will not be judged for their sins, but who have no significant self-motivation to change their behavior.

But what is the church called in the New Testament? The Bride of Christ! The gospel message is in effect a marriage proposal. And just as the prostitute became a queen by marrying the king, guilty sinners have become sons of God by becoming identified with Christ. It is that relationship and our new identity that becomes our motivation, and it is motivation that comes from *within*.

3

Loved and *Accepted*

My son, Bobby, had just graduated from college and was involved in the hard process of finding that first job. Seeing that he was discouraged, I invited him to get together for breakfast to see if I could offer some encouragement and advice.

We had a long, profitable discussion about work, the business world, and interviewing, and he did seem to be perking up. As our conversation was winding down, Bobby said, "Dad, thanks a lot for your time. I really was getting down on myself, but you've helped a lot.

"You know," he said, "one thing I've always known is that you love me. I've never doubted it. You've shown me that in all kinds of ways." I was naturally pleased to hear that, but somehow, it didn't seem complete. I pondered for a few seconds, then God seemed to put a new thought in my mind.

"Bobby, I really do love you—always have and always will—but let me ask you this question. Have you always known that I *accept* you?"

Bobby seemed taken aback. He asked, "What do you mean?"

"I mean there's a difference between love and acceptance. You say you're confident that I love you, but acceptance is something else. Do you know, for example, that I accept you just like you are? That I really like *you*?"

Bobby thought a few moments. Then, in a serious tone, he said, "No, Dad, I guess I really don't. I don't think I have really felt that you accept me." I asked him to tell me about it.

He continued. "I guess I always felt that you would like it if I was more spiritual. You know, if I read my Bible more, or did more Christian activities, or maybe went into full-time Christian work like you did, instead of going into business."

As Bobby shared his true feelings, it stirred up many convicting memories in me. I thought back to the early days of my conversion. Being an extremely gung-ho new Christian, I became heavily involved in personal evangelism. I was very proud of being a "bold witness for Christ." I was sometimes immature and awkward, but my zeal was genuine. Unfortunately, though, I began to consider my lifestyle as the standard to which other people should live. I pressured many people, using subtle and not-so-subtle guilt trips to get them to be like me. I did the same thing to my children. Bobby would come in and announce that he had met a new kid on the block, and had been having fun playing with him. I would look him in the eye and ask, "That's good, Bobby. Did you witness to him?" I expected my 9-year-old son to share an evangelistic message with his friend within 15 minutes of meeting him.

One of the worst and most embarrassing episodes took place a couple of years later. I was by this time in full-time ministry and was attending a training conference. One of the speakers, who had a tremendous reputation as an effective witness, talked about how he had taken his children out to share Christ door-to-door. When I saw all the positive attention he was getting, I thought to myself, "I can do that, too!" After all, I was a bold witness. I wasn't afraid to go knocking on strangers' doors to share my faith! So there I was, with my shy, sensitive, 11-year-old son, walking through neighborhoods sharing Christ with strangers—all to impress other Christians, just so I could receive some of the same accolades that the other man received—while poor Bobby was being scared out of his socks.

I asked Bobby if he remembered that occasion. He remembered it vividly, and admitted that way back then he had determined in his own mind that if that's what it takes to be a good Christian, he would stay out on the periphery and not get too deeply involved. Then, believing in his heart that he wasn't living up to my standards for acceptance, believing that I disapproved of him, he became more and more reserved and distant from me. I could have told him ten thousand times how much I loved him. I could have given him thousands of hugs and kisses, hundreds of gifts. And yet all these demonstrations of my love would have fallen meaningless on deaf ears—*because he didn't believe that I accepted him*.

I finally had the chance to tell him that I was wrong, and to ask Bobby to forgive me for my foolishness through the years. Most importantly, I had the chance to tell him that I not only loved him and always would, but that I accepted him just as he was and that he never had to do or become anything else to earn my acceptance. There was no "if" attached to my acceptance of him at all. I just plain accepted and liked him right now. Our relationship began anew that morning. I also learned a valuable insight: *Love becomes practically meaningless apart from acceptance.*

Having been alerted to this truth, I have since discovered that many Christians are relating to God much as Bobby related to me. Most of them can quote John 3:16: "For God so loved the world. . . ." Yet, they walk around every day feeling that God is sick to His stomach at them because of their failure to live up to His standards. Often, though, it's not even God's standards that they are trying to keep, but regulations imposed by themselves or other people.

There is a certain mind-set that is especially destructive, called the "Phantom Christian." The Phantom Christian is that imaginary person that many of us are continually comparing ourselves to. He is the super-spiritual man who gets up every day at 4:00 A.M. so he can pray for four hours. Then he reads his Bible for four hours. He goes to work (at which he is tops in his field), where he effectively shares Christ with everyone in his office. He teaches several Bible studies, goes to church every time the doors are open, and serves on several committees. He is also a wonderful spiritual leader at home—a sterling example of a loving husband and father, who leads stimulating family devotions every day for his "Proverbs 31" wife and perfect children.

Of course no one could live up to such a standard. Even if some person had the ability, he would still need 100 hours in a day! Rationally, we all know that the Phantom Christian is ridiculous, but the problem is that he is never brought to our consciousness. He is a vague ghost that sits in the back of our minds, creating a sense of failure to measure up. That is the reason why many, many Christians live under continual guilt. For those who believe that the Phantom Christian is God's standard for acceptance, God seems a million miles away, sitting in heaven with His arms folded in disapproval. They don't bother offering prayers because they know He would never answer them.

People in this bondage know well the biblical teaching that God loves them, but they clearly do not believe in their hearts that God *accepts* them. And apart from knowing about and resting in God's acceptance, His love becomes practically meaningless and irrelevant in daily living. I have often talked of God's love in counseling appointments and seen Christians react bitterly to the words. "So what?" they say. "He loves everybody!" What they are saying is that the only love they understand coming from God is some kind of vague, universal, impersonal love.

In many cases, God's true acceptance of us in Christ and the inheritance we have in Him simply isn't taught. However, ignorance of the Word of God is not the only reason for this condition. Many people who know the Bible intimately experience the same thing. I was speaking to the student body of a seminary one time. In the course of discussing the Christian's identity in Christ, I asked a series of questions. "How many of you," I asked, "are as righteous and acceptable *in the sight of God* as I am?" Every hand in the auditorium was raised. "How many of you," I asked again, "are as righteous and acceptable *in the sight of God* as Billy Graham?" This time about half of the audience raised their hands. "How many of you are as acceptable and righteous *in the sight of God* as the apostle Paul?" There were around ten percent of the hands raised. "Now here's the really tough one," I said. "How many of you *in the sight of God* are as righteous and acceptable as *Jesus Christ*?" Only three hands were raised out of an entire auditorium of seminary students.

Mind you, this was not a case of ignorance. These men were attending a fine seminary. Every person in that audience could have defended aggressively the doctrine of justification by faith. They had the truth in their *heads*, all right. But did they have the truth in their *hearts*? It is a perfect illustration of the principle that a person can know what the Bible *says* but not necessarily know what it *means*. I wonder: Would *you* have raised your hand?

I finally told that group of students the same incredible truth that I am laying before you. "I'm going to say this to you straightforward, so there's no chance you'll miss it," I began. *"If you are a true Christian, then you are as righteous and acceptable in the sight of God as Jesus Christ!"* You should have seen some of their faces! I think some of them feared that lightning would strike me on the spot!

What's your reaction? If you are shocked as many of those students were, then it may be that you just don't know who you are in Christ. It may be that you know a great deal of doctrine, but your daily Christian life is still more a burden than a blessing. You may have tried and tried to change your life without success, in spite of all the seminars, books, and tapes you have searched. Whatever your situation, I have great news to share with you. Let's look at some of the fantastic inheritance that we have received in Jesus Christ. It's my prayer that you will never again wrestle with doubts about God's acceptance of you, so that you can go on to discover the immeasurable wonders of His love.

Most Christians, I find, understand the general idea behind forgiveness: God took our sins and gave them to Jesus. But that's only half the message! God also took Christ's perfect righteousness and gave it to us! Second Corinthians 5:21 says, "God made Him who had no sin to be sin for us, so that *in Him we might become the righteousness of God.*" How could I stand up and declare that *in the sight of God* I am as righteous and acceptable as Jesus Christ? Because of what I *do*? No way! It's because of *who I am* in Christ.

The Bible goes to great lengths to declare that righteousness is a free gift that a man receives by faith. Romans 5:17 is explicit:

> For if, by the trespass of the one man [Adam], death reigned through that one man, how much more will those who receive God's abundant

provision of grace and of the *gift of righteousness* reign in life through the one man, Jesus Christ.

Righteousness (a right standing of total acceptability before God) is a *gift*. You don't work for it. You don't earn it. You don't deserve it. Like any gift, all you can do is accept it or reject it. And once you have it, it's yours.

People often respond to me, "I just can't conceive of how God can make me righteous." I reply, "I've got a better question. How could God make Jesus become sin?" Honestly, I have much less trouble understanding how God could make me righteous than I do trying to understand how God could make His perfect Son become sin. But 2 Corinthians 5:21 teaches both.

Those seminary students, able to effectively defend the doctrine of justification by faith, were too timid to state in so many words that they are as righteous as Jesus. And yet to say one is to say the other. The word "justified" *means* to be "declared totally righteous." What hinders someone who knows what the Bible teaches on justification from actually applying it is the attitude that our righteousness in Christ is dealing only with where we go when we die, and that here and now our acceptance is based on our performance. As long as someone thinks this way, he will experience no practical benefit at all from knowing that he is justified in Christ. He will continue dealing with God as if on a merit system, and he will experience the same kind of emotional barrier between himself and God (even though there's no barrier from God's perspective) that my son, Bobby, felt with me. The truth is that God sees us as totally acceptable and righteous in His sight *right now*—not because of what we do, because of what Christ has done for us.

The first application where we will discover whether or not we really believe this is prayer. How do we approach God? How we pray reveals our perception of God's acceptance and what we think He desires from us. What God wants is for us to *trust* Him and His Word—the Word that tells us that Christ has done it all—and to *act* on it by approaching "the throne of grace with *confidence*, so that we may receive mercy and find grace to help in our time of need" (Hebrews 4:16).

Notice that God said, "in our time of need." What is your greatest time of need? Isn't it when you are failing, experiencing temptation, or in the grip of some sin? But if you don't trust that you have been made totally acceptable in God's sight, you will never have the boldness to approach Him. You will linger outside His throne room, trying to find a way to get "worthy" enough to go in. The end result is that you will avoid going to your only source of help (God) when you need Him the most! When could you or I ever be "worthy" to enter the throne room of a holy God on our own? Never. But the New Testament continually and strongly urges us to take full advantage in prayer of what God has done through Christ, "in whom we have *boldness* and *confident access* through faith in Him" (Ephesians 3:12 NASB). Where do we get boldness and confidence? "Through faith in Him." It's all tied up in the phrase to pray "in Jesus' name."

I often ask groups, "What does it mean to pray in Jesus' name?" We've heard the phrase uncounted times. We all end our prayers with it. But nobody seems to know why. Probably the most honest answer I have heard is, "It's a way to end our prayers, like 'Roger, over and out.' " No, it's much more than just a way to end our prayers. To pray in Jesus' name means that we are recognizing two things. First, we are recognizing that *apart from Him* there is no way that we could be accepted by a holy God. But second, we are declaring that *because of Him* and what He has done we can go *boldly* to God *at any time* with full confidence that we will find open, accepting arms! Not because of our own righteousness— because we don't have any—but in *His*. Galatians 3:27 says, "For all of you who were baptized into Christ have *clothed yourselves with Christ*." Because we are *in Him* we are totally acceptable to God!

Now realize that I am talking about *ourselves* being acceptable to God, not necessarily our *actions*. In my identity I am eternally acceptable to Him, but that doesn't mean that everything I *do* is all right. He may put His arm around me, so to speak, and show me the truth about something in my life that is out of line: an attitude, action, or habit. Why? So He can *change* my attitude that is out of line, resulting in a change of action. But at no time is His acceptance of *me* ever in question. At no time does He ever deal with me except in perfect love, acceptance, wisdom, and kindness. Because I am a child of God, there is no occasion in life when He would not attend to my prayer that is offered in faith—that is, in Jesus' name!

Based on my experience in teaching and counseling thousands of people, I have come to believe that the most destructive force in human experience is living under *conditional love and acceptance*. That is, "I love you *if*. . ." The opposite is also true: The most powerful, life-changing power in existence is the message of God's unconditional love and acceptance in Jesus Christ. An unforgettable example is the story of Jean.

Jean had struggled all of her adult life. Married to a career military man who was driven by ambition, she lived in many parts of the world. However, rather than enjoying an exciting lifestyle, Jean was plagued by continual depression. She barely hung on through her dependency upon medically prescribed drugs. But often even they could not give her comfort against the onslaught of depression. On four separate occasions, the emotional pain drove Jean to attempt to take her own life. On her last attempt, she lingered between life and death in a coma for four days. Her husband, tired of the burden of putting up with her, deserted and divorced her.

After her fourth attempt at suicide, she was too frightened to try again. She resigned herself to living, but the depression continued. Alone, Jean returned to the United States to try to establish some kind of life. Here in Dallas, she was invited to a home Bible study that I was teaching. She immediately responded with joy to the good

news and received Jesus Christ. Jean was amazed
as she began to discover what God said about her
in the Scriptures. She hung on every verse that
talked of God's love and acceptance of her and
of her new identity in Christ. Her depressed
appearance, tight nervousness, and labored
movements began to be replaced by smiling
bright eyes, calm relaxation, and a spring in her
step. Jean's total preoccupation with herself was
replaced by a genuine concern for other people.
Soon the depression was only a memory.

I'll never forget the day Jean said to me with a
beaming countenance, "Bob, all my life I've tried
to kill myself—*and I finally succeeded!*" It was
more than a little jarring. She laughed at my
expression and explained, "I was so unhappy for
so long. But now I have learned how much God
loves me, and I'm learning more every day. That
old Jean is dead and gone. She died at the cross
with Jesus. But the new Jean is alive and perfectly loved in Him."

She went on to explain. "All my life I looked
for someone to love me and to accept me just like
I am. I tried to earn my family's acceptance. I
tried to earn my husband's acceptance. I tried
to earn my children's love. I tried to earn my
friends' love. And all along I was trying to earn
God's love and acceptance. But it's terribly hard
to make other people love you when you think
you are unlovable. Only in Jesus have I found
love and acceptance that I can count on forever.
But the wonderful thing is that since I quit *trying*
to get people to love me, I have found more love
than I could ever measure in God's other children."

More than five years have passed since I first met Jean. She has been absolutely free from depression every one of those five years. She is today a joyful, delightful Christian, full of compassion and love. She is a fine, sensitive, and wise counselor to other people who are in the same trap of depression and despair that she escaped through Christ.

Jesus said, "I am the bread of life; he who comes to Me shall not hunger, and he who believes in Me shall never thirst" (John 6:35 NASB). Every human being born into this poor, sin-sick world is born with a craving for unconditional love and acceptance. When we learn to rely totally on Jesus Christ, we find Him to be just what He promised: the total satisfaction for that gnawing hunger and thirst. In Him we find unconditional love, unconditional acceptance, and meaning and purpose in life. All searching comes to an end in Him.

Study Guide

This is the covenant I will make
with the house of Israel after that
time, declares the Lord. I will put my
laws in their minds and write them on
their hearts. I will be their God, and
they will be my people. . . . For I will
forgive their wickedness and will remember their sins no more (Hebrews
8:10-12).

This covenant was promised through Jeremiah
500 years before Christ. What are the provisions
of this new covenant? _____

_____

In the case of a will, it is necessary
to prove the death of the one who
made it, because a will is in force only
when somebody has died. . . . (Hebrews 9:16,17).

When does a will go into effect? _____

When, therefore, did the New Covenant go
into effect? _____

_____

In fact, the law requires that nearly everything be cleansed with blood, and without the shedding of blood there is no forgiveness (Hebrews 9:22).

Why was it necessary for Jesus to die? _____

_____

This is my blood of the covenant, which is poured out for many for the forgiveness of sins (Matthew 26:28).

Why did Jesus shed His blood? _____

For Christ died for sins once for all, the righteous for the unrighteous, to bring you to God. He was put to death in the body but made alive by the Spirit (1 Peter 3:18).

How many times did Christ die for our sins?

_____

For how many sins? _____

What is the result? _____

When you were dead in your sins and in the uncircumcision of your sinful nature, God made you alive with Christ. He forgave us all our sins, having canceled the written code, with its regulations, that was against us and that stood opposed to us; he took it away, nailing it to the cross (Colossians 2:13,14).

How many of your sins did Christ forgive?

_____

> But when this priest had offered
> for all time one sacrifice for sins, he
> sat down at the right hand of God
> (Hebrews 10:12).

How many sacrifices for sin did Jesus make?

_____

For how many sins did He offer this sacrifice?

_____

What did Jesus do after making the sacrifice?

_____

What do you conclude about the completeness of Christ's death for sins? _____

_____

> Then he [the Holy Spirit] adds:
> "Their sins and lawless acts I will re-
> member no more." And where these
> have been forgiven, there is no longer
> any sacrifice for sin (Hebrews 10:17,18).

What does God promise in regard to our sins?

_____

_____

Since our sins are forgiven, is there any need
for further sacrifices for sin? _____

If any more forgiveness were needed, what would Christ have to do? _____

_____

Is He going to come back and die again? ____

> Because by one sacrifice he has made perfect forever those who are being made holy (Hebrews 10:14).

What has Christ done for you through His offering of Himself for sin? _____

_____

For how long have you been made perfect?

_____

> In him we have redemption through his blood, the forgiveness of sins, in accordance with the riches of God's grace.... (Ephesians 1:7).

If you are in Christ, what do you have? ____

_____

Based on the above verses, what do you conclude about the finality of Christ's work on the Cross in regard to your sins? _____

_____

In Christ you have forgiveness of sins. Christ died for *all* your sins once and for all, and as a result you are made perfect forever in His sight. Our prayer is that through this study you will rest in the finality of the Cross, so that you will experience the reality of the resurrection.

Classic Christianity

For every vibrant, fulfilled Christian, there seem to be nine who are "doing all the right things" but still feel bogged down, tied up, or burned out.

Drawing on his own struggles and years of teaching and counseling experience, Bob cuts right to the heart of the matter to confront the question of *why* so many Christians start out as enthusiastic believers and end up merely "going through the motions" of the Christian life. Discover the way back to authentic Christianity—the kind that Christ had in mind when He set us free.

Get back on track in experiencing true abundant living. Life's too short to miss the real thing!

Bob George, founder and president of Discipleship Counseling Services, is the counselor and teacher on "People to People," a daily biblical counseling program broadcast live via satellite on radio stations from coast to coast. Bob has authored numerous Bible study books and has a passion for communicating God's grace to hurting men and women.